GROWING CANNABIS HANDBOOK

How To Grow Your Own Cannabis: From Seed To Smoke

CALEB EDWARDS

Table of Contents

CHAPTER ONE

How to Grow Cannabis

How To Grow Your Own Cannabis: From Seed To Smoke

Determine the Legal Status

Identifying the legal status of cannabis cultivation in your state, as well as the maximum number of plants you can grow, is an important first step before beginning your marijuana garden. Only two cannabis plants are allowed in some states, while up to 16 are permitted in others. The laws in your area are constantly changing, so keep up with them.

What You Should Expect to Pay

The cost of starting a cannabis farm includes everything from the plant's nutrition to grow lights and gardening tools. Start-up costs can run into thousands of dollars, but if you're looking to grow marijuana at home,

Decide on a Site: Indoors or Out?

Growing marijuana indoors is a popular choice for new growers for a variety of reasons, including convenience and privacy. Both indoor and outdoor setups have their advantages and disadvantages.

Marijuana Farming in the Outdoors

Even if nature is doing most of the work, growing cannabis outdoors can be a challenge (i.e. providing light, water, and soil, although you can use your own pots and soil as well). In order to successfully grow cannabis outdoors, you must take into account a much larger number of factors and be situated in the proper geographic region. As a general rule, those who live in climates that are not equatorial, Mediterranean, or temperate may have a difficult time growing outside.

Cannabis grown outdoors, on the other hand, offers a unique sensory experience and many people prefer the effects it can produce. Because of this, if you live in the right climate, have access to the right amount of space, and are familiar with your local weather, growing cannabis outdoors can be a breeze. As long as the weather doesn't change drastically, all you have to do is watch your cannabis plants grow and give them some TLC along the way (e.g. a little pruning).

.

Outdoor Planting Strains to Consider

Indoor and outdoor cannabis cultivators should consider cultivating the following strains:

feminization of the early queen / early skeleton

• Autoflowering Gorilla Glue #4

• Dutch Passion's Skywalker Haze is a must-have for any Star Wars fan.

- Feminized Nikki and Swami's Lemon OG

Feminization of Steve's Dream Queen

- CBD Feminized Mango

Indoor Cannabis Planting

When it comes to starting out, indoor growing is the best option because you can control all the variables. Indoor cannabis cultivation does not require much more than soil or a coco coir-and-organic-nutrient mix, 400- to 600-watt lights, a grow tent, and a few pots.

Indoor Growing: The Best Strains

If you're a novice to indoor cannabis cultivation, the following varieties are recommended:

• Aurora borealis (NL)

In the case of Skunk #1,

- Dream Blue

- Blue Cheese/Cheddar

- Blueberry

- The OG Kush

Also recommended for novice indoor growers is the use of autoflowering strains and ruderalis strains.

A Greenhouse as a Tool

The advantages of indoor and outdoor cannabis growing can be combined in a greenhouse.

CHAPTER TWO

Cannabis can be kept in a safe environment to reduce pests by covering greenhouses to create a true dark time (though not as much as an indoor grow).

Additionally, the natural light that greenhouses provide allows the cannabinoids and terpenes in the cannabis plant to fully develop. In addition to using fewer resources, growing in a greenhouse requires fewer lights and fans than growing indoors. Other plants can be used to hide the cannabis in an enclosed area, making it easier to avoid detection.

In spite of this, greenhouse crops are susceptible to the seasons and require a significant amount of natural light. Additionally, it is difficult to regulate temperature and humidity. However, a greenhouse is an option worth considering for those who are interested in outdoor growing but do not live in a suitable environment.

Decide on Your Growth Strategy

You can choose from a variety of cannabis growing media. The following are some of the most common methods of growing marijuana, along with some of the benefits and drawbacks of each.

Soil

Many people prefer the smell, taste, and effect of outdoor cannabis to that of indoor cannabis due to the natural soil and sunlight that can be used in outdoor grows. The legality of outdoor cultivation is debatable, and there are numerous other factors to take into account.

Indoor growers can also use soil, and many prefer it because it is a natural source of nutrients and you don't need to add too many extra nutrients from other sources. Many gardening supply stores carry high-quality soil.

Advantages

• Cannabis has a better flavor, smell, and effect than tobacco. •

Drawbacks

The weather.

There are legal concerns.

• Pests.

• Thieves.

Animals in the wild.

Maintains a delicate balance between water and light.

• Only two harvests per year are possible (depending on your climate).

Overall, the experience was difficult.

In other words, Coco Coir.

A natural fiber derived from the outer husk of a coconut is known as coco coir. Essentially, it's a hybrid of hydroponic and soil growing. It's a great starting medium for new gardeners because it can be used with or without soil.

Advantages

• High water retention capacity.

Drainage must be reliable.

• A lot of space.

By providing nutrient water, you are reducing the need for your plants' roots to search for food.

• The pH range of coco coir is 5.2-6.8 — ideal for cannabis cultivation.

• Reduces the risk of your plant being attacked by pests, fungi, and other harmful pathogens.

As long as it's prepped correctly, it can be reused for your next growth cycle.

Drawbacks

Coir bales are often treated with chemicals in order to prevent them from becoming infected with harmful pathogens, so read the label or look up information about your coir on the manufacturer website to ensure that the chemicals will not interfere with the plant growth cycle.

• Increasing the plant's calcium, magnesium, and iron levels requires coco coir-specific nutrients.

It's possible that some coco coir has been rinsed in saltwater, in which case you'll want to make sure it's been rinsed with fresh water.

This means that you'll have to supply the plants with their own food supply.

CHAPTER THREE

Hydroponics

Mineral nutrient solutions in water are used to cultivate cannabis hydroponically. It is common for the plant to be placed in a pot surrounded by an inert growing medium (eg. perlite, vermiculite or clay aggregate) and to have a nutrient solution flow through the inert material and directly into the plant (continuous-flow solution culture). Keeping the plant in a reservoir of nutrients is an option in some cases (static solution culture).

Advantages

• Massive and potent yields.

Drawbacks

• Specified nutrient needs. •

An understanding of various strains is necessary for the best possible development.

• It is necessary to use aerated water.

More suitable for more experienced growers.

Aeroponic

An aerated chamber is filled with fine drops of nutrient solution, similar to hydroponics, to keep the plant's roots submerged in the solution. A fine mist of atomized nutrients is sprayed on the roots at regular intervals.

Aeration-grown plants require less nutrients and water than hydroponically-grown plants, but unlike hydroponically-grown crops, can be transferred to soil without causing shock.

Advantages

• High-yielding processes.

Drawbacks

• Costly at the start.

• Constant monitoring is required.

A lot of time and pressure.

Aquaponics

Using hydroponics and aquaculture, aquaponics is a combination of aquaculture and hydroponics. Aquaponics is a symbiotic system in which aquatic animals' waste feeds the plants growing on top, and the plants remove toxic waste levels from the water. Despite the fact that aquaponics systems have been around for a long time, it is debatable whether or not they have been perfected until recently.

Advantages

Minimal use of water

• There is no need for any plant food whatsoever.

The use of chemicals is minimal to non-existent.

Insects and diseases have a harder time invading.

Aquaponic systems are excellent for the growth of marijuana plants.

Drawbacks

• There are fewer plants because the area is smaller.

Large amounts of electricity are generated.

• Requires a lot of attention.

• More complicated, so there are more places where things can go wrong.

• High prices.

Step-by-Step Instructions for Growing Marijuana from Seeds

In order to grow marijuana from seed, there are a number of steps to take. Once you've chosen your marijuana seeds, you'll take the plant through every stage of growth, from germination to harvest.

Germinate

Wait for a taproot to emerge after spraying two to four sheets of paper towels (kitchen towels) with water. Then, place a seed between the towels and on a plate. Keep the temperature between 70 and 90 degrees Fahrenheit.

Transplant

Once the seed has germinated, place it in a small pot of soil or another suitable growing medium. It has two leaves that open outward from the stem when it is a seedling, so that it can begin receiving sunlight.

It's at this point that you begin to notice a miniature cannabis plant. At a humidity level of 60 percent or higher, seedlings need to be kept at 77 degrees Fahrenheit. After the leaves have emerged, cannabis prefers a light cycle of 18 hours of white light per day. Nitrogen-rich fertilizer should be used at this stage.

You'll need to move your seedling to a larger pot at this point. When the roots of the seedling have grown to the point where they can no longer fit in the pot, it's time to transplant it. At this stage, cannabis plants are putting on significant amounts of weight because they are absorbing an increasing amount of nutrients and carbon dioxide.

At this point, you can also perform some important checks. One is performing a plant sex test. Two white pistils will begin to form in the female plants. Pollen sacs are produced by the plants that are sexually mature. Before it pollinates the females and ruins your harvest, remove the plant if you see these sacs.

Maintain a humidity level of 50% to 70% and a temperature range of 68-77 degrees Fahrenheit. In a 24-hour day, there are 18 hours of daylight and only 6 hours of darkness. 125 Watts of light wattage. This stage is skipped entirely by Cannabis ruderalis, which moves on to the next stage of development (flowering). Phosphorus (P), potassium (K), and nitrogen (N) (K).

In the midst of blooming

When the vegetative plant's trichomes begin to form, you know it's ready to produce new buds or flowers (little white hairs that are the powerhouse of cannabinoid and terpene production).

The plant should be moved to a larger container. 12 hours of light and dark are required for this stage in the plant's life cycle. Indicas flower in six to nine weeks, while Sativas take between 10 and 14 weeks. Most growers limit their flowering period to a maximum of 14 weeks.

Make sure there are no light leaks during the flowering stage at night. Hermaphroditism (hermying), "hermying," "hermied," or "hermies" can occur even in feminized varieties when the plant is stressed by light leaks.

Keep the temperature between 68 and 77 degrees Fahrenheit,

with a humidity level of about 50%. The plant needs no more nitrogen (N), but it does need more phosphorus (P) and potassium (K) in its diet (K). Flush the soil with distilled water once the plant is in its final week of flowering, and then stop adding nutrients.

Harvesting

Chop and dry your plant once it has reached maturity. The plant must first be chopped at the appropriate time. The plants should be harvested when 70 to 90 percent of the pistils have turned brown, according to some sources.

Others focus on the trichomes' changing color from white to amber to brown. Harvesting should be done when the trichomes are half amber (50 percent) or more. If it's too obvious, it may also be too soon (but can produce a more energetic effect). Cannabinoids lose their potency if they become too brown (although some may prefer slightly less psychoactivity).

CHAPTER FOUR

Drying

For seven to fourteen days, keep your cannabis plants in a dark, dry place away from direct sunlight. When the plant stem snaps when you bend it, your cannabis plant is ready for chopping into smaller buds for jarring. This is a critical step, as a bad drying process can lead to mold and mildew in your cannabis.

Curing

Cannabis that has been chopped, pruned, and dried can still be used, but it will not be at its best. Use a mason jar with a tight-fitting lid (no more than 3/4 full) to store your cannabis. Open the jar once a day for two weeks to a month to allow the marijuana to breathe. Sugar and chlorophyll are broken down by this process, resulting in a more flavorful and well-defined product.

Tips and Tricks for Growing

There are a slew of effective methods for ensuring the

success of your cannabis plant. Even a dying cannabis plant can be saved. Here are a few tips to help you get the most out of your cannabis plants:

• Keep an eye on the weather, particularly the light and temperature.

• Make sure there is enough water available.

Use this information to better understand the cannabis plant's life cycle.

• Pick at the right time of year.

How to Keep Your Own Marijuana in the House

Proper storage of your homegrown cannabis is critical to preserving the quality of your crop.

Storage in dark, cool areas is ideal for airtight containers. To preserve the potency and freshness of your cannabis, keep it away from direct sunlight, high temperatures, and moisture.

How can I help you?

In terms of time, how long does it take a marijuana plant to mature?

The average time it takes to grow a marijuana plant from seedling to harvest is 16 weeks, but this varies depending on the strain you're growing and the medium you're using.

The question is whether or not it is legal to grow marijuana.

Make sure you know the legality of growing marijuana in your area before you start with seeds.

Whether to grow marijuana indoors or outdoors is a matter of personal preference.

Many novice growers find that growing cannabis indoors is more convenient because they have more control over the environment. Pest infestations and harsh weather conditions are just some of the dangers of cultivating cannabis outdoors.

Use your medical marijuana card to learn more about the plant's myriad uses. In our virtual clinic, our doctors are ready to meet with you and get you started on your treatment plan.

THE END